Valley of Shadows

BY Mary

and her daughter,

Nancy Weston

*In memory of Mary,
a tribute to her bravery,
courage and her strength.*

Valley of Shadows

Last night at midnight, Mary decided she would go home. She stood up and put on a knitted coat over her nightgown, then put on a robe over that. She placed a photo of her eldest brother in the pocket of her walker and hung some dish towels and a dress on its frame. As she headed for the front door, I quietly got up, stepped into my Uggs, grabbed a jacket and put it over my pajamas. Following mom as she made her way to the front door, I asked, "Where are you off to, Mom?"

She replied, "I'm going home! I'm getting out of here!"

I've been here before. As she opened the door, I turned on the porch light so she could see whatever her weary eyes would allow. As she lifted her walker over the threshold and onto the concrete, I came in close to provide any needed steadying. She rolled forward on the walkway and remarked how dark it was.

I said, "It's the middle of the night, Mom. It will get darker the farther away you get from the ...."

She finished the sentence, "...lights."

I said, "Yes. That's right."

It was also cold — a dank cold as it had rained heavily for four days and nights. Feeling the lick of cold on her legs, she turned around to return to the front door. I stepped aside to allow her passage but stayed close in case she needed help up the single step to re-enter the house. I suggested that she stay in the house until morning. Then I would help her get home, if she would help me find her home.

"You know where I live!" she snapped, even as she appeared to agree that staying till light was a good idea. She went to her room.

Mom was always so independent and self-reliant – not by design as much as by necessity. Life had dealt her a difficult hand, but she played it as best she could. I never heard her complain. She always thanked God for providing what she needed. But I think secretly she took pride in her resilience and resourcefulness, even though her choices for survival were not always, in fact not often, conventional or entirely wise. Nonetheless, she would make do, get along. She drew on her endless cleverness and found a way to make a life for herself. I didn't help her much in the beginning.

I was a precocious child and fairly early, I found it easy to keep one step ahead of my mother. As a teenager, you might say I was a bit wild and certainly willful. Late in my teens, I ran from the dastardly house of my father straight into the challenge of survival — unprepared, unaware, and seething with rage. I tasted of many pleasures and adventures and did what I wanted. I thought little of what concern I might be reflecting on Mom.

At some point my mother found herself out in the world, on her own, also unprepared and unaware, naive, and financially unstable. I shored up her finances because she had no margin for error. To start, I made sure her car was serviced and capable of taking her to and from work. I would treat her to a new outfit or some small luxury – at least by her standards. I contributed money for the holiday meals she always prepared — she extended an open invitation to anyone who wanted to come. Not much really. She did well at her job and was promoted. Her employer appreciated her diligence and knew she was someone who would never assert her true worth, her value, to them. So she earned a modest income and great respect for over twenty years.

When Mom retired, I bought her home. I paid the taxes; she paid for her groceries and utilities. When she needed a new car, I bought her one; ditto a new mattress and washing machine. I visited, kept in touch, looked after her to make sure she was "getting along." My career had me travelling extensively, much of it outside the country. But I always managed to get home to visit and make sure she was okay.

Mom and I were both products of a set of truly unfortunate circumstances. She stayed, but I ran. And I kept running until I felt safe from the mire — the mire that sucked her down and into quite a precarious situation with my father. I did offer to take her with me. She chose to remain. I couldn't. Had I stayed; I'd likely be writing this from prison where I'd be serving time for patricide. I had to go.

So now, helplessly lost in this strange land of dementia, I am not surprised that she is frustrated and angry. Uncharacteristically and somewhat pathetically, she often takes to self-pitying. It is as if all the governors and guards through which she filtered her angst into something more cheerful and proud were gone. Now it is time for her to display her true colors, in a way. But that is not entirely true, it's just true in a certain way. Because the courageous person who held back her tears, her fears, and her sense of disappointment, who put on that jolly front, was also fiercely brave. She always hid the frightened child who never figured out how to stand up for herself; instead, she disguised all the angst. We all do it to one degree or another. I confess, I never realized the depth of her internal trauma until now.

It has been a long time since anyone thought of me as gullible. But in the case of my mother, I have succumbed to her self-sufficient, independent act (as it were). In all these years, I never realized there was a small child inside her who felt unloved and powerless. Maybe it was convenient for me to rely on that façade — it gave me more comfort as I was off living my life, making my choices and doing what I wanted with only obligatory concern for her. Her mask was my license to be distant.

The truth is that our lives were very different. We had little in common. She disapproved of many of my choices and I questioned some of hers — there was some mutual self-service in our physical distance. At arm's length, she didn't have to fuss with me, and I didn't have to silently shake my head as much. There was no doubt we loved each other very much. Separation helped us keep our relationship as free from judgment and argument as possible — distance worked for us.

If you have never observed a person succumbing to this cruel disease, you cannot imagine how excruciating it is — for the afflicted and for those who love and care for the afflicted. But when I turn my eyes to the sky and take a deep breath, I realize that the world can be brighter and hopeful. She cannot turn her eyes anywhere and escape the anguish of her delusions, the torment of being surrounded by liars, thieves, cheaters, and a cast of hundreds who menace her. My greatest torment is that I cannot rescue her from this hell.

It is ironic that I, comfortable with a bit of distance all those years and showing up to intervene when needed, find myself helpless and distanced by this disease, unable to arrive within the dimension in which she now resides and do much for her at all. For the first time in my life, I am utterly powerless. Watching from the sidelines, I am unable to effect change, to help her, to do anything to avail her of salvation. The best I can hope for, day to day, is to remain a friendly specter in her delusions rather than a bad guy. In this role I can be there to offer a hug, some consolation, understanding... and occasionally attempt to explain and give context. At times I am the bad guy, evil, a criminal in the drama. I must be shunned, plotted against — sometimes vehemently prayed against that my devil be cast out and I be defeated. In the role of bad guy, I am her jailer, her chief tormentor, while she is fairly regularly in escape mode of some form.

As I study, research and inquire, I am struck by the total lack of direct communication about the horrors of this cruel brand of dementia. I refer to the glossy coat of generalities and vague explanations that are offered about what dementia is, in particular those related to Alzheimer's disease. There are several reasons I want to tell this story. One is to share my brave mother's battle with this affliction; another is to share exactly what it is like. I wish I had understood more before I had to face Alzheimer's in a state of confusion and self-doubt. In hindsight, I would have understood that unsettling events were a product of the disease at work, not some fault of mine or my failure to be the best caregiver I could.

Let's set the *Way Back Machine*: October 1957 in southwest Los Angeles, California. The concord grapes ripe, it was my happy task to climb up the amazingly sturdy arbor to cut clusters from the thick, tangled vines. The grapes were dark and sweet. I would squeeze the insides into my mouth and drop the skins, which were thick and a tad bitter. In the early fall bounty of large, thick clusters, my pilfering made no dent whatsoever in the harvest.

Being small, I could lay in the vines, invisible but to God above. I loved watching the blue sky in safety and relative quiet, even though it wasn't allowed outside of harvest season. The harvest was destined for cheese cloth sacks that Grandma sewed every year. On the big, redwood table in the center of the arbor, the kettle sat. As the grapes came off the vines they were rinsed and placed in the sacks. The sacks were twisted and twisted until all the juice was extracted and only twigs, skins, and bugs were left. Yes, bugs. Bees, spiders — lots of insects love grapes. Even after you rinse the grapes, the bugs remain trapped, tightly held within the clusters. In the end, after the twisting is done, the bugs become leavings in the sack. Ultimately, the kettle is cooked to a boil and the liquid is poured into canning jars. The smell is thick, sweet, and pervasive. The vapors penetrate the sinuses and find their way into memory, indelible. Hot, steaming paraffin wax closes the mouth of the jar; a cap and lid are screwed down tight to secure the still-warm juice. The jars sit in rows waiting for the "pop" of the lid being sucked down over the paraffin as they cool.

That smell filled my every breath, kind of tickled the back of my tongue — a sensation I would later recognize in the first sniff of a sweet wine like port or sherry. It is slightly different in a dry wine and different from grape to grape. It made me want to swallow the saliva that formed, but there was no real taste, it was more like a tease of things to come. No doubt my love of wine and fascination with how each variety pairs with salmon, cheese, chocolate, chicken, or beef are rooted in the autumn rituals in that arbor. Indeed, I love the traditions of wine, the popping of a cork, the aromas, and tasting as much as I value the memories of harvest.

The jars were stored in the cellar on a "shelf" cut into the dirt wall. There they sat until it was time to open one and drink the wonderful juice inside. The cheese cloth — stained red purple by the skins, sticky and stretched out of useful shape — was tossed. The kettle was scrubbed and put away. The vines were trimmed, and the twigs and cuttings raked up and burned: another wonderful aroma. It was a glorious time that made me feel rich and wonderful — as if the world were full of promise and the harvest of grapes a signal for me to feel blessed. I think Mom and Grandma felt it too.

Grandma was the wife of a farmer who had raised seven children on her own after her beloved husband died. She had great soul but her eyes were fixed on heaven above — that's the best way I can describe her. She was strong, courageous, a great cook, and a survivor — and very gentle and accepting. She was my very own oak tree rooted, giving me shade and comfort while reaching high above, somehow connecting me to heaven. At the same time, she was deeply rooted on Earth: Growing, reaping, and cooking things and giving them as gifts of life and affirmation was what she was all about. So she loved the grape harvest. Mom did too. Mom doted on her mother, and I doted on both of them.

The harvest was a time of togetherness for us three. We did this special thing as a team, a unit. From my earliest memory, I was part of it; I was on the team. I have no siblings, so it was just me, Mom, and Grandma. Grandma, that good oak tree in the middle of our lives and Mom and me always in her drip ring. There would be one more harvest, then Grandma would be gone. When she died, it felt like that great tree was hacked down, leaving a large hole where she had stood and the earth, empty of her shelter, ravaged by sun.

Mom suffered Grandma's loss directly and immensely. After the initial shock waves subsided, Mom and I formed a new team in preparation for surviving the storms to come. I could never be Grandma for her, but I sensed there was a large role for me to play in her life. Grandma had told me that after she left us, I would need to look after Mom. It was a heavy mantle for a twelve-year-old, but one I intuitively knew was mine to wear. I have always known that was my purpose; that God sent me here to take care of her.

My mother was the youngest child of seven. Her father died when she was just four years old. To her siblings she was the one last burden in the coming struggle: unnecessary, unwanted, helpless, an encumbrance. Mom felt like an excess liability and that her siblings, sometimes even her mother, wished she were more of an asset — or at least less of a weight — during their battle to subsist long before any of them had options to live or to thrive. She was never able to lay down that impact: She carries it into this maddening world in which she now resides.

How do we know if a person has Alzheimer's disease or dementia? Only an autopsy can confirm it. Every form of senior cognitive decay is a form of dementia and some dementia is Alzheimer's. Some say that alarming personality changes, combativeness and, yes, meanness are indicators of Alzheimer's. But I don't think they know for sure. In fact, they really don't know very much. This is frightening because baby boomers are approaching the age where this becomes acutely relevant. I have seen many statistics, but the one that sticks in my mind is that one in ten people aged 65 to 85 will develop a form of dementia. After 85 the ratio jumps to one in two. Terrifying. Even if these projections are overstated, it is still an alarming reality considering the wave of baby boomers approaching these thresholds.

I never worried about this because never for one minute did I think my mother would have dementia. She went well into her nineties with a sharp mind. While opinionated and on a different wavelength than I, she was aware and articulate. She drove a car until she was 91. Then one day she came to me and said, "I don't feel confident when I drive now. I am uncomfortable and I don't want to hurt anyone. I don't think I should drive anymore." It was a thoughtful act of great courage, in my opinion. I was somewhat in awe of her, as I always have been. I became her chauffeur, which greatly inconvenienced her and robbed her of her freedom. But she was very on point that it was time and never wavered.

Her thinking was clear, rational, unselfish, and well considered. She was able to put aside her own convenience and independence, something she had always valued, and think responsibly. I was confident we were way past a point where the loss of cognitive ability would become a problem that affected our lives. We knew families who had been hit hard by this cruel disease; it was heartbreaking. I was grateful that particular cup seemed to have passed our lips. Little did I know we were headed into a storm. It would arrive without warning one night in July when Mom was just shy of ninety-six.

People tell you that dementia is about forgetting, but that is only part of the story. Dementia is also about making strange connections and forming demented versions of memories of this or that — twisted inventions with which the mind must grapple. And, in an effort to make sense of the insane constructs of what's left, the mind goes on high alert searching and suspecting causes for its confusion. The afflicted individual ends up concluding that everything has turned foreign, crazy, and wild. Paranoia and mistrust of everything and everyone become the norm. Over time, all havens of comfort are lost, leaving only fear, anger, and resentment. *This* is the fright of Alzheimer's.

In 2011, Dark Castle Entertainment released a movie called "Unknown." Based on the 2003 French novel by Didier Van Cauwelaert and published in English as "Out of My Head," the movie stars Liam Neeson and Diane Kruger. It is about Dr. Martin Harris, a man who is the victim of a plot to rob him of his identity after an accident that nearly killed him while he was visiting a foreign country. Fairly fractured and helpless, Harris twists and fights to figure it out, asserting his beliefs about what is actually going on. He battles to keep a grip on reality as circumstances appear to prove him insane.

The movie character, Martin Harris, is intelligent and highly resourceful – and of course, correct. There is a plot and he is its victim. Now, imagine that he is all of that, but unable to articulate what he believes. His faculties cannot coordinate his responses. He is driven insane, his perceptions out of whack. I imagine this is what it's like to wander into dementia: It must be terrifying, exasperating, bewildering, perpetual, and deteriorating.

First, let me reiterate: No one can know for sure that a person has Alzheimer's disease until after death and upon examination of the brain in autopsy when the presence of the plaque associated with Alzheimer's can be confirmed[1]. My mom has dementia. Many of the professionals who come in contact with her or review her records believe she has Alzheimer's. There are variations in how the disease manifests, but there are norms in the path to dementia. And while someone may have a very

---

[1] At the time of publication, new detection techniques are available to detect the disorder.

passive experience with dementia, what is most often associated with Alzheimer's is rarely passive.

Regardless, the mind does not go quietly into that dark night: that twisted landscape. No, it fights and scratches to make sense of the fragments of understanding and faculty that remain, while fermented with an echo of what was... before. Deeply entrenched feelings, propensities, and perspectives surface and latch onto the fragments. Every day I am amazed by the inventive ways Mom twists up little pieces of memory seemingly with fears or forebodings she has harbored all her life. Perhaps it comes from the loss of understanding and context for routine, day-to-day occurrences. The mind relentlessly grapples with the confusion and strives to give it meaning. In the end, it generates deformed, distorted versions of reality to make sense of the fragments.

To the observer outside that chaos, it makes no sense at all. The versions of reality are irrational, convoluted, negative and, often, very ugly. And there is absolutely no reasoning with this disease. The ability to connect dots fades until it is nonexistent. Any attempt to help the individual make a rational connection will get jumbled up and can make matters worse — you will appear argumentative and combative, which is not helpful. Debate will likely evoke anger or withdrawal and, ultimately, generate fear as talk progresses. In fact, as memories slip away, impressions are simultaneously imprinted at a primal level.

Sometimes, when I am very strong, I allow the child in me to observe her face and see her fear and frustration as she navigates this scary terrain. Once in a while she moves into a space of real reality. In those moments, she knows. I may come in to see her and she will have a look of pain on her face. I'll ask her how she is. She will reply, "I'm so confused." My heart is shredded. At times when she has behaved badly, she will come to me and say, "I apologize. I don't know why I said those things." And I know in that moment, she is there, with me, once again. And then she disappears back into the shadows.

It is excruciating to watch someone you love so much be reduced to such a state, to know that she is trapped inside a place of such torment. It is excruciating to have to stand helpless by her side knowing there is nothing I can do to slow the disease, halt it, or alter it in any way. My only recourse is to pull back some from my daughter perspective and put the adult out front to protect me — then I am less vulnerable. The alternative is to be overcome and collapse in a puddle of sadness and pain where I am utterly useless to her.

My mother has always modeled bravery for me. There is nothing notable about doing a thing or facing a thing if you are not afraid of it. I remember exploits as a very young girl in which I appeared to be fearless. But, in fact, I was too stupid or naïve to comprehend the depth and breadth of a rational fear. I just plowed ahead drunk on a sense of invulnerability.

All children are born with a sense of immortality and impenetrable resilience. Eventually we come face-to-face with the concept of mortality and the fact that it will touch us in our own time and under the circumstances life uniquely brings to us. Coming to this realization is one of the most important aspects of growing up and shedding our innocence. Until it materializes, children carry on as if the rules that adults apply to adults have no bearing on their fates. It is a wonderful time of life.

I recall clearly that in my secret heart, deep inside my being, I knew that if necessary, I could fly! I knew it to be true as I knew that the sky spread itself above the earth…. Okay, the sky doesn't spread itself above the Earth, rather all around it. And it isn't a sky, but the reflected light of our sun diffused in our atmosphere — but that is the point: As a child I existed inside my evolving perceptions. It was quite a while before I began to grasp the pale, blue bubble, my mortality, and the harsh truth that is gravity. To the casual observer, I appeared to be a courageous child. I was bold perhaps, but not brave.

In reality, you cannot exhibit courage until you face fear. Courage is what we muster to marshal forward in spite of our fear. My mother, on the other hand, spent most of her life in a state of fear. Yet day by day, year after year, she marshalled forward — and this is the essence of bravery.

Mom may have experienced that perfume of indestructibility and unfettered aspiration for a time while roller skating. As a child she was an avid roller skater — she did it with passion and aplomb, defying gravity and injury for a number of years. Evidence, perhaps, that once she did feel that childlike freedom from the brutality of our mortal destiny and flawed nature. I prefer to think so — and I hope so, because to live and never know that sense of immortality and imperviousness is a lesser form of existence, I am sure.

To die having missed this *and* the dawning of mortality – this fullest circle of enlightenment – seems to me to be a huge deficit in understanding life, appreciating life. They are paired experiences that go hand in hand. The sense of immortality and the realization of mortality is a crucial dichotomy and one of the clauses in the definition of the human drama. The Greeks understood this and claimed it is what the Gods themselves envy.

My realization came to pass when a close friend, seeking adventure with abandon, pushed fate one too many times: She died in a freak accident in her early twenties. It was like an alarm clock signaling "time to grow up and do the math." It rocked my world.

Mom's world was all about born again Christianity and another form of immortality. It is very human to seek a rationality that permits belief in our immortality. It is an escape clause from the unpleasant alternative idea that life ends with our last breath and that is simply that – so far as the individual is concerned. We want to believe that the world cannot go on, that the universe will cease if our consciousness is not part of it. And it may be that there is an after-life. Perhaps there is a heaven and a hell. Maybe it is a good thing to behave in this life as if there will be a judgment day. But this thinking can also cheat the individual of the value and importance of every moment of this life.

I believe Mom's enchanted childhood experience of invulnerability was brief and limited. I believe it was followed by a foreboding sense of impending doom and failure. I believe she embraced Christianity as a means of extending her sense of immortality and combating her fears. And I believe that she lived her life awaiting the end of life on Earth. For her, Armageddon, the tribulation and judgment day, loomed in the wings, not front and center in her world, but still omnipresent and threatening.

The doom was held in check by her faith in God and her belief that living a Christian life of piety, service, and propriety would help her overcome the evil that shadowed the world and reap her reward in heaven. This sustained her and bolstered courage. And it gave her license to think of this life as a prelude to another and better life. All my years I observed that to Mom, this life had less meaning, less importance, less value than the one that would come.

But now, she lives among confused sensations and braiding slips of memories mutating into a terrifying, surreal existence. She has lost control over the specters of fear and dread. Everything is frightening and everything is dreadful. It has even shaken her faith in God, but it has not wrecked it.

When I was young, my mother would always tell me to be brave and to be bold; to go out and learn, experience, and make my own way and to not follow others. This had a profound effect on my life. I took her advice, and it has made for an exceptional life. I am very grateful for her guidance. However, I don't think my mother expected me to translate her advice in the ways that I did.

In her version of my life, while out there being bold and experiencing things, I was *supposed* to end up marrying a wonderful man, preferably a preacher or missionary or, at the very least, a deacon in a fine church. I was to have children so she would have grandchildren. I was *supposed* to become a born-again Christian, play the piano and organ, direct the choir, teach Sunday school, and pray for the sick. Ideally, I would love to cook, wear aprons, bake angel food cakes, and love shopping for dishes and cookware. I would wear full skirts and get permanent waves. I would display doilies under lamps and on chair backs, taking pride and pleasure in washing, starching, and placing them.

I have been married, divorced, married again, and widowed. I have no children. I am not a born-again Christian. I can carry a tune with my very ordinary voice but play no instrument. It is not in my nature to perform on any stage, including a church; I don't even attend church. I appreciate the skill and artistry that go into making a doily, but I don't use them. I love to cook but don't bake much. As such, on many levels,

I am a great disappointment to my mother. And if all this were not a sufficient indictment, there is more: I am a committed same-sex partner.

Marie and I have been together for over twenty-five years. We have worked hard to build our relationship. Marie is gay. I am the worst nightmare of fundamentalist Christians and Republican right wingers: A bisexual who sees life as blessed with choices and love extraordinary no matter where it is found! I chose this relationship with Marie.

I have always had a propensity for women. And as I said, I have been married twice. I have had wonderful relationships with men. I like men. They can be fun sexual partners and they can be interesting. They can also be jerks — a lot like women, based on my experience.

I don't see a lot of difference between men and women, except for the plumbing. I do acknowledge that there are more large and strong humans who are male rather than female. I have known strong women, large women; and I have known weak and/or men of small stature. I have known women who were mechanically inclined and those to whom math and engineering came naturally. I have known men who were brilliant cooks and men who's forte in engineering was the construction of fabulous garments. We all live in and out of the subtleties associated with norms, averages and bell curves. To me, every individual has a unique profile that evolves over a lifetime to render each one a special, extraordinary, and one-of-a-kind being.

I have observed different sets of learned behaviors and the consequences of those behaviors over a lifetime. But at the core, I believe that it is healthy to be human first and then a gender. I believe we are far more alike than we are different, and that focusing on our human-ness – first and foremost – is key to getting past many of the differences that divide our society. We humans are at once essentially the same and brilliantly unique: This is part of the commonality that is human.

We are all male and female to some degree. Some are more comfortable identifying with one or the other. Others prefer to rely on the labels that society places on our genitalia, which can constrain us from being who we are first and foremost: human. With human as the starting point, the plumbing is more like hair color or being right or left-handed. Gender and other aspects of individuality follow that which is first. Reversing the order can invite a little weirdness regardless of our plumbing.

Marie and I are very different: opposites in most traits. It has been a distinct choice and endeavor to embrace each other for our differences and capitalize on our commonalities. It did not happen without effort and dedication. We have had bad years and better years; now it is really good. We have both grown and evolved through the years to become who and what we are today: a valued and valuable collaboration and companionship!

I am who I am, at least in part, because Marie stood by me while I bounced around figuring things out: principles, character, preferences, style, and aspirations. I cannot speak for Marie, but I can say she has truly blossomed over the course of our relationship. Marie has a voice to die for and impeccable good taste. She has a very distinct style, courage, and loyalty. She is also smart, diligent, faithful, and hard-working — she is my partner in making a life together and making this house our home. Mom struggles to see her in that light or to give credence to our relationship.

From time to time, Mom has been downright insulting to Marie. In the beginning, Marie gave back in kind. As Mom aged, and Marie gained confidence, she seemed to mellow, becoming more forgiving and tolerant. Mom, on the other hand, tends to say she hopes I will remarry. Explaining that I am in a committed relationship with Marie and not interested in any other relationship only made her a muffled version of angry.

It is clear that what I am and who I am does not measure up to Mom's expectations. She loves me and would lay down her life for me — of this I have no doubt. There is a vast difference between love and like. Mom loves me but does not like me. I have been aware of this for a long time. Loving her includes embracing that loving me, without liking me, is probably the best she is ever going to be able to do. Many do not have that much. I am good with it.

Early in the journey to loss of cognitive power, Mom determined to blame things on Marie. It is a fairly obvious retying of connections in terms of remembering and understanding nutsy things happening in her mind. Mom sees my partnership with Marie as a wrong thing – so if there is to be a villain, it works well for that to be my wrong partner. Marie stole from her, said horrible things to try to make her leave: "Marie doesn't want me here" or "Marie wants my room for herself." Everything was Marie's fault; she was a bad person, a villain. I knew these things were not true. My core self could not believe them. So in the beginning I would attempt to reason with Mom.

But over time more villains appeared in her landscape. Some of the early manifestations were weird accusations levied at this person or that. First it was Marie who went into her closet and stole her clothing! It made no sense whatsoever, but to Mom it was real. We'd go downstairs and search in Marie's room as Marie sat there graciously watching the exercise. Finding nothing, we would go back upstairs. In the beginning that ended it, but eventually this became a constant theme. And after Marie had done that and done that, she needed another villain: me! I must be stealing her clothes and, later, selling it to fund my lifestyle! Or maybe it was one of the women at her church. There was no reasoning with her.

Now, Mom believes that we steal from her and sell her clothes. And that we have a small band of people living in our downstairs, many of them children, who are supplemented by the money and things we routinely steal from her. All of these delusions torment her; some of it terrifies her.

There is a little boy who searches through her drawers and takes things and a little girl who climbs up in the bookcase and throws things on the floor, smashing them. And why won't I stand up for her, protect her from these awful people? I participate in conversations with beings I cannot see. I scold them, warn them to stay away, chase them out of the house. Why? I hope it will make her feel protected, defended, and safe. I don't know what else to do.

Sometimes in the night they form a circle around her bed and chant curses at her. Why do I allow this? She has extended delusions with intricate backstories involving a long list of characters. The delusions can take bizarre and grizzly turns and often involve punishment and retribution. Nothing we do or say changes those beliefs. That is the nature of this brand of dementia.

I can turn on the light in the night, lay on the bed with her, and hold her till she falls asleep to keep her safe from the awful people. But I cannot prevent them from entering her dreams or being there when she wakes. I stand helpless watching it all go down. Eventually, I am no longer trusted to be her nighttime protector. I am as bad as they: I allow it, tolerate it.

Sometimes I can hardly breathe. I feel each breath as a labor, chest heaving a bit to absorb enough oxygen to keep me calm. "There are no people. I am not a bad guy... not my mother talking. This is my job right now. I am all she has. I must breathe and try not to dwell on it... just breathe."

The delusions are very real and even seductive — because in them, Mom can drive a car, owns a house, is often called upon by powerful and influential people for counsel... she takes care of herself, walks, dances if she wants... . All so much more compelling than the reality I offer her in which she is crippled, limited, nearly blind, nearly deaf, and unable to make sense of her world. For me, there is no winning. I am better off rolling with it than attempting to dissuade or fight against such a powerful intoxication.

Rolling with it means that sometimes it is best to just walk away. When the conversation becomes pointed, accusatory, or disturbing, or when she asks me to take her to some nonexistent place or find someone who is a construct of her delusion, it is better to defuse the moment and move on to something else, if at all possible. At times, the only way to break the spell is to leave the room. If I do so and wait about ten minutes, then return, she is less agitated or on to some other topic. But not always.

For example, today she asked me to take her to the "store on the mountain" where "they have wonderful things for very little money." Now if I knew where this place was, I would take her! But I have no idea. And, of course, it is possible there is no such place or that she has composed it from several concepts of a place fused to become the "store on the mountain."

In her new-version memory, she believes we have shopped there before and that I know how to get there. But that is not the case. There may have been a store that I cannot connect from the description she provides. Regardless, I don't know how to get there whether there is an actual store versus a delusion. But she says I have been there before. I'm the one who took her there in the first place and I know she loves to shop there! Why won't I take her there now? She is shaping to accuse me of keeping her prisoner, controlling her and preventing her from doing things she wants to do. I can deflect for a while. In this type of situation, counseling professionals all advise to deflect, change the subject, point her attention away to something that will captivate her awareness and cause her to let go of the fixation on the "store on the mountain."

I tell her that I can't take her to that store, but I'm going to JCPenney and would she like to go shopping there? She says yes. We get in the car and head toward the highway to the next town over where JCPenney is located. Before we get to the highway, she starts bemoaning the fact that it is so far away... she wanted to go just down the road. I explain that there is no store just down the road. All the stores are downtown and JCPenney is in the next town down the highway. She is unhappy and I'm unable to defuse the conversation, so I ask if she wants to turn around – she does.

On the way back, she asks if we can go to Valmont or Wickers or…. I say, "Walmart?" And lucky for me, that is the name of the store she was searching for. In that instance, I was able to apply reasoning to sort the words she was using to determine the word she was seeking. We return to our town and to Walmart. We walk around for a while, looking at things. She needs to sit down so we go to the pharmacy department; she sits next to a nice woman and they chat for about ten minutes. After buying nothing, we return home to fix lunch. She seems content with that.

The day had been a busy one. We were active and she probably walked about half a mile in total. For a 98-year-old woman with a mended hip, osteoporosis, and scoliosis, that's a distance. After a good lunch, she went to her room and took a nap. Sometimes when she is asleep, really asleep, she loses her sense of space and time. She awoke and asked to get up.

"Momma, you are in your room and you can get up if you want to get up. Do you need help?"

"No," says she. "But you didn't get me up for breakfast!"

"This morning you had breakfast. Then we went out for a ride, remember? Then you had lunch and took a nap. It is early evening now."

"You people don't know anything. I don't know why you can't keep it straight. I want my breakfast!"

"I am happy to make you breakfast, Mom. I'll go to the kitchen and get started."

I did. After a while she came out to the dining area, sat down, and waited for me to serve her hash browns, two soft-boiled eggs, and a glass of milk. She ate hungrily and happily. I finished the laundry while she ate so I could be close if she needed anything. She likes to fold clean laundry, so it also has the portents of a happy activity for her.

Space and time are highly distorted. Sometimes she is in the dark, its 2:00 a.m. and she's flipping on lights because she can't see and is convinced it is morning and time for breakfast or to go to church. On other occasions, the sun is shining, yet she thinks it's time to get ready for bed because it's nighttime.

They talk about "sundowner" syndrome. It is when the patient is fairly lucid in the morning but as the day wears on, he or she slips out of touch and the delusions get worse. I found as many days when that was not the case as when it was – so I can't comment on this syndrome. I can say that nights were the most difficult for us. As sleep becomes more and more rare the nights are active with wakening, motion, and delusions. Perhaps this is a version of the syndrome.

She has lived in our home for twelve years, and yet is convinced it is an elder care home – and not a very good one since we never know what time it is. She has lost the lay of the land. Sometimes she will come and ask me how to get to the kitchen when just a glance over her shoulder would reveal where it is. At other times, she is upstairs but thinks she is downstairs and needs to get upstairs, or vice versa.

Sometimes she thinks she's been displaced: Every morning now for months she's been claiming that in the night, Marie, I, or other "people" moved her downstairs, and she is frantic to get back upstairs to "her room." In reality, her room is on the upper floor and she rarely goes downstairs anymore, except when we need to work out some spatial confusion or search through Marie's closet. She goes down in her chair lift and tries to connect with how the house is laid out and where things are – when she thinks they are somewhere else. But she is most always upstairs and always sleeps in her room.

We are struggling to keep her safe since she gets up in the night more and more and often wanders around. I always hear her walker hit the hardwood floor just outside her room, which is not far from mine. I worry that some night when I'm exhausted, I'll fall into a deep sleep and she will wander herself into trouble and I won't know it. They call this a wander risk. My mother has late-stage dementia and is a wander risk.

I never thought of Mom as having a label or being in a category. She had her own style of dressing and it was sweet and wonderful. She made some of her dresses as money was not plentiful. I admired that, too. She wore flowers and ribbons in her hair, kept it short to mid-length, with a perm and always softly curled, combed, and feminine. She never consumed alcohol or smoked. She didn't go to motion picture shows and didn't play cards. She read her Bible through at least once every year; she could quote it, find anything, and answer all the Bible-related questions on Jeopardy. She was modest, kind, thoughtful, and selfless.

Yet she always had a scheme working to get something she really wanted... she set aside little pockets of money, saving for the big "get." She would share it with me with glee — telling me how much she had saved or what a deal she had gotten on something. She marched, as it were, to her own tambourine. And although it was a march to which I didn't relate, I admired her for her individuality. But in other ways, she was completely programmed and utterly brainwashed.

She took as gospel every word spoken by television evangelists. If she was hooked on their charismatic qualities, they could do no wrong. She sent money to at least fifteen televangelists and their causes, plus a couple of lobbyists who promised to get her money from Social Security because she is a "notch victim" entitled to special benefits. She did all of this with small, regular checks, typically in the amount of $35. Altogether she gave away at least one third of her income, faithfully, for over thirty-five years. I estimate that she – who has virtually nothing – gave away over $200,000, piece by piece to people who have private jets, Armani suits, and lavish homes. Okay, not all of them are like that, but many are. You'd think they'd be ashamed. But con artists live by a different code than the rest of us. I never tried to stop her because I knew she was buying a parcel of self-esteem, and I knew she needed all of that she could get, or money could buy – if it could. Besides, it was her money. So now she has nothing at all but Social Security, Medicare, and me as her cushions in life.

Over the past two and a half years, I've had to take over her finances. When she would get confused, she neglected to pay her phone bill and AT&T would shut it off. After her hip surgery, she had a lot of medical bills to deal with and it overwhelmed her, to say the least. After the surgery, it took help and more money to enable her to make the great comeback she has. Slowly, over the months, I'd say, "Mom, do you want me to take care of that for you?"

Or she'd say, "Can you help me with this?" I would, of course. It would be a mess. So, again, I'd say, "Do you want me to take care of this for you?" I put all her bills on autopay. The bank provides great records and there are no more worries about late payments. Her finances are now in a state of calm control. But she doesn't necessarily remember asking me to help or remember what I explained to her about the money. She perceives that I have taken her money to run "my" house. She can go to the bank and get money whenever she wants. We live in a very small town. Everyone at the bank knows her and have watched her deterioration over this arc of dementia. They work with her and help her as much as possible. When she goes to the bank, she typically takes out a hundred dollars. Often after she comes home, she "loses" the money within a couple hours — then accuses someone of stealing it. In fact, she has put it away somewhere safe and can't remember that she did or where she put it.

Writing checks is not viable anymore — and it is somewhat of a relief. She was writing checks to her favorite "causes" and would overdraw. I put an overdraft card on her account; she has run it up over a thousand dollars. As the months pass, she feels more and more cut off from her money. I can explain it to her, but she cannot understand. She twists what I tell her into some weird disaster or thinks I'm saying I need her money – she cannot process my telling of what her money is spent on or how the money works.

Like many aspects of her life, money has become a bit of a prickly business. There is really no way for this to work out well. I do what I deem appropriate and brace for the consequences. The things she says, I am told, are not to be construed as the words of my mother. And in truth, I know Mom would not say the things she now says if her brain were healthy.

It is difficult to hear these things every day, be accused constantly, without letting an arrow zing into the core and hurt at least once in a while. I confess, I lose my temper sometimes. And when I do, I always say things I wish I had not. Then I beat up on myself, feeling like the slime that snails leave behind. The only remedy for this is to forgive myself.

It takes a bit of work to shed the snail slime and revert to my role as daughter. One way to do this is to apologize for my outburst because I absolutely could not help it at that moment. It was spontaneous, unrehearsed, a reflexive reaction to my pain. Nonetheless, I am very sorry that I spoke with malice and disrespect. I clean it up by apologizing. She doesn't always understand or remember exactly what happened. But I must do this for myself — it is part of self-forgiveness, cleaning up from the inside out. Maybe you know what I mean.

I have help on Wednesdays. A caregiver comes for ten hours and I can get away to do whatever I need or want to do. But I could not leave Mom with just anyone, so I pay extra to be picky: about 150 percent of the state-supplemented programs for in-home health care services.

Otherwise I would worry the whole time, in which case I might as well not bother going out. I look for the most intelligent, informed, trustworthy, and caring person I can find — and I am happy to pay more.

The only thing that keeps me sane (if I am) is the knowledge that on Wednesdays, I can leave this nightmare and get some fresh perspective. I am saddened that Mom can never, ever take a break from her imprisonment.

It's not that the professionals are wrong when they counsel to deflect, avoid, and distract in the face of impossible scenarios such as the "store on the mountain" or going home, or whatever havoc is playing out at the time. It's the answer that someone comes up with when they work a shift. In a memory loss program, caregivers work six-, eight-, even ten-hour shifts. They must deflect, avoid, and distract over that period. Then the new shift comes on and the demented patient starts all over with a new caregiver.

When you are *the* caregiver 24/7, deflection always comes back to bite you, often with a vengeance. The patient with dementia is disturbed, not stupid. Inescapably, another way you fail her is when she catches on to the game — then I am just cheating her with my delays, my avoidance and distractions, and she gets really mad about it. Understandable, and probably foreseeable. But in the beginning, I grabbed onto things as I sought a way to cope with the lunacy. I learned that the dynamic is different for the 24/7 (or in my case, 24/6+) caregiver. It always comes back around to make matters worse in the end. I have found it is better to try to go with it than to deflect.

I developed a new strategy: facilitator. When she wants to go to the "store on the mountain" or anywhere else, I tell her I'll take her if she will tell me where to go. We get ready and get in the car. I roll out of the garage and ask, "Which way should we go, Mom?" She indicates a direction and off we go. It usually ends in our circling around until we return to our house; it is frustrating for both of us. But at least I can be something other than her jailer. I am helping her get where she wants to go.

She wants to go home, which takes many forms, but it is always away from here. Sometimes she has bought a house and her niece Florence is coming to live with her. Sometimes she believes that she lives somewhere else and has just come to our home by accident, or manipulation, or malicious intent… or whatever on a given day. Even shopping at the store on the mountain often has to do with buying something for her move to her home. Marie brought home boxes and I got packing materials so she can pack. This is a very good plan: When she is anxious to move, I remind her she hasn't finished packing. She'll start packing some things, then lose interest, and move on to something else. There was one box on her bedroom floor; now there are three in various stages of being filled with this and that.

Once in a while, she tells me that the movers are coming to get her stuff and move her "home." Sometimes it fades over a morning. But other times it is an enduring delusion. When the movers do not show up, she becomes agitated: Where are they? Why haven't they come? It becomes problematic.

One time, she decided that the "mover business" was on a street she could see from her window. She insisted that the man had agreed to come and help her. In the late afternoon, we got in the car and drove to that street. I slowly cruised along the residential cul-de-sac, hoping she'd realize there was no business there. Then she sees a huge, white Ford 250 truck in a driveway and proclaims, "That's the place!" I assess my options and, invoking my facilitation strategy, I pull up behind the truck, go around and help Mom out of the car. With her walker, she heads to the steps leading to the porch. A nice neighbor opens his door and listens as Mom tries to explain what she wants. She asks if he is the man who promised to move her. The man looks over her head and at me. Without saying a word, I look back into his eyes. He understands and begins talking to Mom about how he used to have a moving company, but he's retired now. He tells her that she can look in the phone directory for a moving business. Mom seems satisfied with his explanation and turns toward our car. As she turned away, the man mouthed the words, "My mother has dementia." I will always be grateful for the kindness of that man and many others who seemed to grasp what was going on and rolled along with her — kindly, graciously, mercifully.

Sometimes "going home" is to a house where her mother, my grandmother, lives, and Mom also lives. She becomes frustrated because she can't get there. Sometimes she is married to (a youthful sweetheart named) Bill. They have a home together and she needs to get home to him and his son. At other times, home is where all her siblings live and await her arrival. I think this is actually pretty accurate because I think that in her mind, home is really heaven where she believes all her family await her. Home is also a return to an earlier time when she was in command of her life and it was not this constant, unsolvable puzzle. It is a time when she drives, walks, sees, makes her own decisions and runs her own life. At that time, all her siblings were alive and playing a part in her life. But of course, she cannot get there from here, at least not by any means I can provide her.

I am not a neurologist. I know a lot about anatomy and physiology, but I have no specific education in how the nervous system or brain functions. Nonetheless, I do observe the deterioration day by day and track certain affects as they mutate and manifest. For example, in the beginning there is a weakening of decision making — either confusion or corruption of the decisions themselves. Memories of recent events are clouded and pieces of older memories stream in to fill in the blanks in the short-term recollections. Identification becomes significantly more dependent on distinct cues. For example, she will recognize someone by her hairstyle, and a change to that style is confusing. An individual is described by his shirt color rather than by name... at first. Later, the ability to remember someone from one encounter to the next becomes more compromised. Eventually each meeting requires linking people to memories still in the brain. But the links seem entirely broken and, in the end, their identity may be lost altogether.

Things that were learned long ago — working a zipper, tying shoes, using a brush — slip away, and so we have Velcro shoes and snaps on clothing. It is a constant task of observing the deficits and trying to compensate, anticipate, so she can maintain some independence. And everything is a double-edged sword. We go out and get her new clothes so she can "work" them more easily. But they are not familiar, so she constructs that we have taken all her other clothes and sold them, and now she has these clothes that are not hers and she doesn't like. She has turned against green, red, and yellow. Her favorite colors have always been blue, purple, green, and pink. But now, it's all about pink: If it's pink, it works. If it's another color, on the spectrum of blue and purple, it can work. Anything else is a crapshoot on any given day.

One morning, Mom awoke steeped in a delusion in which a very good friend of ours had passed away and left her house to Mom. I didn't correct her, but I said I hadn't heard anything about it and was pretty sure that our friend was okay. Mom was adamant that our friend had died in the night and that they had read her will and she had left her house to Mom. The delusion persisted after breakfast, and she would not be diverted or diffused. After we got dressed, she wanted to go to her new house. I loaded her in the car, and we drove to our friend's house. Mom got out and headed to the door. Our friend came out to greet her and Mom, taken aback, didn't seem to know what to say or do. She decided she wanted to return home.

As the disease progresses, words become more elusive and she struggles to describe certain situations or objects. Later still, sentences are composed from a shrinking vocabulary of possible words, dwindling monthly until reading is impossible because the words do not make sense. Conversation becomes an overwhelming challenge. Interestingly, sound bites, lifelong phrases, and familiar words deeply ingrained remain. She inserts them at the most appropriate moments, giving the impression that she is more in control than she is — if you are with her all the time you know better. "How are you, Mary?" "Pretty good for an old lady." She has said it thousands of times in her life and it remains ready on her tongue, long after pulling that phrase together via reason and selection would have become an insurmountable challenge.

One challenge is making sure she gets enough protein. I work at ensuring she has a minimum of 35 grams daily, even as her appetite takes surprising turns. She used to eat so very well. She was aware of good nutrition, eating plenty of fruits and vegetables and avoiding fats and sweets. But the teeth are all false now, which adds difficulty. She has osteoporosis and scoliosis. With bones very porous, the teeth cannot be pinned or clamped as well as they might – so chewing is a regular adjustment. We go to the dentist every few months — and sometimes every month — to shore up her ability to chew. Also, she is adamant about tending to some personal hygiene herself. While she is reluctant to let me take charge of things like her teeth, I do give her baths, roll up her hair and comb it every day, and put the battery in her hearing aid and fit it into her ear. But she clings stubbornly to her dental regimen. From time to time, if she hasn't cleaned her teeth adequately, some gunk will prevent the clips from sinking in and holding them. Or a small piece of food will lodge under the plate and hurt. It is a relentless battle for the ability to bite down.

Fresh vegetables are almost out of the question, so we eat an inordinate amount of canned peas, carrots, corn, and lima beans — far less nutritious than broccoli, asparagus, fresh beans, and other high-fiber, complex carbohydrates. Fruit is also a fading possibility. Biting an apple, chewing the fiber of an orange until it can be swallowed, masticating peach skin are all growing obstacles. I peel and cut them, and we do what we can. I prefer to avoid canned fruit which, high in sugar and low in the valuable nutritional components, can adversely affect digestion and elimination.

She's a Scot so she loves her roasted beast and potatoes. Beef, pork, chicken — cooked until it's falling apart — and mashed potatoes are always hits. But no matter how tender, the meat is requiring more chewing until the juice is gone; more and more often, the hulk is left on the plate. Lately I've been making corned beef hash, finely ground, with fried eggs – it goes over big time. It may not be healthy, but it is protein. My goal is not so much to prolong her life as to ensure she gets the nutrients for a fighting chance at walking, talking, moving, and functioning. Without protein, her systems will quickly deteriorate and fail. Whereas a healthy adult can live without food in the range of 30 to 60 days, Mom's frailty would lead to loss of function and death within a short period of time. We struggle constantly to keep her as close to one hundred pounds as we can — it doesn't take much for her to slip to ninety-five, ninety-two.

She loves ice cream and I'm happy to give it to her anytime she asks for it — same with breads, pastries, and other treats. But she eats potato bread because grainy, seedy, textured breads are hard on her teeth. Peanut butter is a favorite — also protein, so we eat a goodly amount of it. Avocado on toast with a little mayo, salt, and pepper is another favorite.

There are also protein drinks I make with fresh fruit and protein powder. She doesn't like Ensure because it is too sweet; she will drink high- protein strawberry Boost. I keep a supply and it is a regular supplement. Yogurt is also a tasty source of protein and sits easy on her stomach at night. If she goes to bed without protein in her stomach, she will not sleep. And if she eats more solid foods near bedtime, gas traps in the eddies and lagoons of her sagging digestive system — and she wakes in pain.

Sleep is another challenge. She does not sleep for extended periods of time at all anymore. She sleeps for a couple of hours and then wakes to go to the bathroom. She may sleep again for an hour or two, or maybe not. She may wake in a cogent state or wake in a dream, unable to shake it. She plays it out while awake — and it can become the basis of a new delusion.

Over a year ago, she fell out of bed in the night and got badly bruised. I immediately purchased bed rails to keep her safe, but she hates them. She does not see them as a safety feature. To her they are prison bars. At times she has tried to wreck them by ripping, pulling, pushing, and yanking at them. For a tiny person, I am amazed at the strength and power she can summon in a demented state of anger. The bars held, but she hurt herself in the process. She begged to be free of them, so some months ago I lowered them, and there they remain.

I used to get up with her every time she needed to get up: I would lower the rails, get her walker, and make sure she was stable as she set out for the toilet. Even though this meant that I got up every few hours every single night, it was the only way I could be confident that she would be safe.

I asked her doctor how I could help her avoid another serious injury like the broken hip (that precipitated the dementia). He said, "Never let her get up in the night alone, for that is when she is most vulnerable to a fall." When I did sleep, I slept easier knowing that we were doing all that could be done to protect her when she was most vulnerable to a fall. The hip surgery is really the crux of this situation.

Over two years ago, one night around midnight, I awoke to a pounding on the floor. It was a dull sound as it was muffled by carpet. But it was a wrong sound, so it woke me. I went to Mom's room and found her on the floor with feet twisted in a way they would be if her hip were compromised — I knew. She wanted me to help her get up. I called 911. She had awoken in the night, probably groggy, and tried to get out of bed. She must have twisted her feet, lost balance, and fallen. With the force of her feet twisted and the weight of her body, she split her porous, fragile femur.

In the emergency room, the doctor showed us the X-rays. He said they recommended surgery to repair the femur, but that at her age the odds were not in her favor. He said that once under anesthesia, there was a 50 percent chance she would not survive. And if she did make it, there was a 50 percent chance that she would not thrive and could die soon. And if she managed to thrive, there was only a 50 percent chance she would ever walk again. He asked if we understood this; we both said yes. Then Mom signed a DNR (do not resuscitate), saying that she was ready to go to heaven and be with Jesus, and would not want to be brought back if there were a problem. The surgery was performed thirty-six hours later upon the arrival of key surgical components. The fact is, we did not comprehend the meaning of those statistics at all.

When she awoke, she was mad as a hornet. She could not comprehend that she was in a hospital, had surgery to mend her hip, or that the nurses, doctors, and therapists were there to help her. She told the physical therapist to "… get away you devil!" She was sure she was in an insane asylum and being held prisoner, when all she wanted was to do her laundry and get a glass of milk from the kitchen. She was not herself, not herself at all! I was horrified and fretful.

I went back to the hospital the next morning and saw that they had tied Mom in the bed (something they are not permitted to do, which I did not know at the time). She was frantic. They had wrenched her disabled left arm uncomfortably to tie her so. I was livid. She cried to me that she would be good if I untied her – I did so immediately, then went to find out why she had been bound. I was told she was insistent about getting out of bed all night and it was a way to keep her safe. Soon it was branded in my brain what that meant, and I also began to try to keep her in bed and safe. As the nurses had a whole ward to attend, they could not constantly watch her, so containing her was for her own good.

But I couldn't allow her to be tied in the bed – not my mother! She was frantic, so I moved into the hospital to keep watch over her. They would say, "Give it time. It may wear off. It's the anesthetic, especially with bone surgery. It has this effect on the elderly. Give it time." I clung to those words because this was not my Mom. She scratched me, hit me, ripped off my glasses and threw them across the room. It was horrible. "Give it time. It may wear off." I needed to believe in those words.

It took about a year after the surgery for me to put it together: There was a 50 percent chance of dying under anesthesia because anesthesia is *very* hard on the elderly. A 50 percent chance of not thriving and dying after the surgery would not necessarily be a physical failing – but a mental failure, with catastrophic consequences in the end. But the chance of walking if she survived — that we could tackle, and we did!

After five days she was moved to the hospital's Extended Care Unit (ECU). She was still not herself, but a little improved. The ECU was managed by a great, granite rock of a woman named Bonnie. She explained that they had a plan to help Mom recover. She said, "Give it time. The nuttiness may wear off. It's the anesthetic, it has this effect on the elderly. Give it time." She said the words I needed to hear, so I listened.

The plan was simple: sleep, eat breakfast, work, rest, ingest protein, work, have lunch, work, rest, protein, work, rest, have dinner, work, sleep — and do it all again the next day. Every activity was therapy for recovery. Getting to the dining room was work, as was going to the ECU hairdresser, and the exercise room for therapy, and toileting and hygiene — all opportunities to practice activities of daily living. This was the recovery plan, and everything would work together to return her to her life – if she would cooperate.

I explained this to Mom. I could tell that she was grasping it, especially the "returning to her life" part. The plan included Mom going to a nursing home for a while after twenty days in the ECU. I told her that we had to work diligently for twenty days to prove that the nursing home wouldn't be necessary and so she could come home with me instead. She got that! And so we began implementing our plan. She was eager and strove to do whatever physical therapy was required. She persevered and I was proud to be her partner in the effort.

Some patients were not willing or able to do the work because it hurt, which was sad and understandable. Also still affected by the anesthesia, they didn't fully grasp the consequences, I am sure. But without the physical work, the healing and walking would not happen. Many were destined for the nursing home and would never leave. At this juncture family and friends are a godsend — you are fortunate if you have someone cogent and on your side. Mom was determined and she had an army on her side: me, Marie, and many friends and well-wishers encouraging her along the way.

I spent twelve hours a day with her in the facility; we rested, ate, and worked the whole time. We took a "roll" in the gardens every day and went out to the farmer's market on Wednesdays. We would buy blackberries and cream and share them with everyone in the ECU. She received more cards, letters, and flowers than anyone ever in the ECU; friends and fellow churchgoers visited. Her pastor came on Sundays and gave her communion. I read her the twenty-third psalm every night, and then we said the Lord's Prayer together before I left: *...yea though I walk through the valley of the shadow of death, I will fear no evil.*

She hated their coffee, so every morning I brought her a stiff cup of French roast with lots of cream and sweetener. Actually, she didn't like their food, either — so it added to the incentive to work hard to get home. As the days passed, the drugs wore off and she returned to her old self and to be my Mom. Every day she was brighter and more rational — it was a hopeful time.

The hospital corridors were very long and ran the full perimeter of the facility. Besides the physical and occupational therapy, we would go to the exercise room and use the equipment and the cafeteria after it closed to do all our exercises again. Everyday I'd roll her to the far end of the corridor from the ECU and she would pedal herself back, pulling with the repaired leg. I cheered her on and encouraged her to pull harder with the left so she would stay straight. If she got too crocked, I'd straighten her. As we approached the ECU, the staff who knew her also cheered her on, smiling and laughing with her, impressed by her determination and courage. She was the star of the ECU! To the surprise of many — but not Mom and me — on day twenty-one we went home. I always knew she was not going to a nursing home, ever.

She was prescribed home visits from an occupational therapist and a physical therapist to ensure a satisfactory transition. Marie and I had built our home for her, for this inevitability. She had a walk-in tub and there were no steps anywhere, except to go downstairs — and for that she had a chairlift. Everything was wheelchair accessible; her toilet was high and had grab rails for easier up and down. When the professionals were satisfied, we were all set to continue the battle at home, they signed her off as "transitioned."

While Mom was still in the ECU, I had looked for a caregiver who could help us out at home. I found a retired Certified Nursing Assistant (CNA) whom I felt was a fit. Though she hadn't kept up her certification, she was knowledgeable and capable on many levels. In no time I was comfortable leaving Mom with her. They became fast friends and it was great.

I could leave Mom alone for short periods and go to the grocery store without concern. More often than not, she wanted to go with me to town to do an errand, shop, or whatever — just for the drive, the outing. It was good for her to get out and see people, to walk, chat with friends or people she encountered, and buy things she wanted, like greeting cards.

My Mom is the last of her siblings — her four brothers and two sisters have passed away. That makes Mom the matriarch of a huge family that at last count numbered almost two hundred — my cousins, first, second and otherwise: her nieces and nephews and their families. As matriarch, she believes it is her role to keep up with all of them — and it is her pleasure. She knows them all and keeps track of children and grandchildren: their birthdays, comings and goings, schools, jobs, everything. She calls and writes and keeps up with cards: at least six to eight a month. And they love her right back — she is beloved.

But soon after she came home, she began struggling to keep track. She buys cards, but often forgets to send them. I find them in various stages of completion: yet untouched, addressed but illegible, or in the return mail as undeliverable. Sometimes she forgets to put the stamp on the envelope. She may lose cards she has bought and claim they were stolen or think she has sent them. Of late, sending them herself has become just impossible. Her CNA has to help her, or I do, if she is in the mode of letting me help her.

With me her fight for independence is most fierce, as if she has to prove to me that she can take care of herself. Over time, this has mutated toward resentment. After all, as she loses her independence, as she becomes more reliant, her dependence transitions to me: I am the one she must rely on. That I would be a source of resentment is fairly rational and understandable under any circumstance. But this is deeper; at times, it veers to a sort of irrational resentment.

More and more, I am just the bad guy. For example, I take her in the car and pretend I don't know where she wants to go. Then I bring her home again, where I keep her prisoner in order to get all her money. I am an awful person who is insensitive and mean and won't let her or help her do the things she wants to do. She tells people that I "slap her around," and she has called the cops on me several times. When they show up, they quickly get what is going on and ask if they can help.

Almost always now I am her dead sister, Ellen. Her daughter was killed in an automobile accident. She has a little daughter, Nancy, my name, but the child is very young and looks like I did when I was young — but I am not her daughter. I am mean, cruel, a thief, a liar, and a cheat. Even my strategy to roll with it and be the facilitator is now failing. All she thinks about is how to escape my clutches.

Thriving is not always about a physical condition of heart and lungs —the mind must also thrive. The mind is everything and if it fails, then all is vulnerable, everything, every single thing. Mom survived the surgery. She got back to walking with her walker and could even go short distances without it. But she didn't thrive after the surgery. Instead, she endured a slow corruption of her brain that I didn't see or understand until it was clear I had lost her to demented delusions. There would be no reversal, no salvation, no cure and no hope — only a gruesome end farther down this nightmare of a road.

The morning after the surgery was a harbinger that I did not comprehend. Even if I had, I was in such denial that I could only grasp at any straw offered and cling to the belief that her bizarre behavior was due to residual anesthesia: anomalous, temporary, an aberration, the consequence of urinary tract infections, dehydration, an antibiotic — anything that would be a better end than dementia, than Alzheimer's disease.

The first year was full of progress and hope. We had fun and worked together toward the goal of her walking again without a walker or other aid. In the fall, we made seasonal decorations, homemade soup, meatloaf, and chili. We planned for Thanksgiving, which was all about the dishes she had taught me. Together again, we prepared everything and welcomed company, celebrating all for which we were grateful and, that year, there was much! Her odds as told to us in the ER were bleak: 50% x 50% x 50% = 12.5%. But Mom had beat the odds, she had triumphed and emerged victorious. We rejoiced!

Christmas, though quiet, was lovely. We had all the usual and traditional meals, events, and rituals. One such ritual on Christmas Eve was Mom's recitation from memory of the "The Night Before Christmas" complete with animation and charm. She had done this on Christmas Eve for as many years as I could recall; it was a tradition. That year she couldn't remember it all, which was understandable considering what she had been through. I got out the little book and we read it together, which was even more special! Marie took photos of us and I am so grateful, because that was the last time Mom was able to do it so cogently, so coherently.

As dry leaves that before the wild hurricane fly — a warning to the sensitive and observant that trouble is in the wind. There were a thousand tiny indicators I overlooked as the days came and went. Now when I look back, I see them, see how they fit into spaces in the puzzle that was forming piece by piece. But what child, given any choice, would opt for going down a path of anguish and unknown, scary prospects? Did others around me? I'm not sure, but the morning I called the doctor and shared some events of the moment, he said calmly, "Nancy, your mother has dementia." He said it as if it might have been obvious to him, and that it was only now rising to the surface in my consciousness.

I am writing to tell my peers that if you think Alzheimer's disease simply robs a person of memory, then you fail to grasp what that means. It is the mechanism by which the life is stolen, the "self" is stolen, leaving the individual in a world that no longer makes sense and is filled with paranoia, suspicion, confusion, fear, torment, and horror.

The afflicted helplessly behaves in ways she would otherwise abhor and say things she would never, ever say. You are left to watch from outside that world, unable to intervene or help. You are forced into the role of unwilling, unwitting accomplice in the unfolding drama. No matter what you do or how hard you try to maintain your part as offspring, friend, or hero, you are highly likely to be cast as a villain, the archenemy in a dwindling life.

If you are faced with such a problem, what are your alternatives? To not assume the job of caregiver? To put your loved one in a memory loss program or nursing home and visit? This may sound like a thesis suggesting that you can't win, so don't engage in the battle. And it might be — it just depends on you.

I can say that being a caregiver for a parent with severe dementia is best undertaken if your love is unconditional. The disease will try the most avid and unqualified devotion. If you have any baggage, it will test you severely. It will demand that you put it aside, abandon it, early in the journey. This is because a person with dementia is unable to deal with your baggage or be your parent anymore. He or she is consumed with trying to cope with a world gone haywire. Believe me, whatever s/he did to you, or you perceive s/he did to you, s/he will be paying a worse price than any sentence meted out by a cosmic justice league. It is really important that you consider that *you* will pay a price as well.

Several months ago, I determined that I couldn't take it anymore. With the bed rails lowered, she was free to get up all night long — and she did, every night. She was probably up and about more than she slept. I had not slept much in almost three years; I was exhausted. Now she had taken to going to the exits of the house and trying to escape. It became about vigilance to keep her safe from her regular attempts to leave the house, not just visits to the toilet and back.

For example, I might have to pull on my UGGs and follow her outside at one a.m. so she can figure out that she needs to return to the safety of the house. You might say why allow her out, why not alarm the doors? I will tell you that alarms have been recommended by everyone, but she believes she is imprisoned as it is. An alarm would only upset her. Letting her leave, if that is what she wants to do, is a far less combative option. She is free to open the door, go outside, walk as far as she can, then turn around and go back inside — all her choices. I'm just there to turn on the lights, stay the walker on the concrete, and watch over her in the night.

I am far more wounded these days. I am no longer her daughter and there are no more moments of affection between us. She yells at me frequently and says things simply to be mean as she fights back against her perceived captor. I'm having more and more trouble keeping her eating and elimination on track. She is incontinent and wears protection.

Even so, "accidents" are more frequent, and this is a strain on both of us. She is present enough to feel humiliation. It can be tricky if she feels compelled to participate in the recovery. I have no problem with cleaning up — just as she did it for me when I was a child. It is testing, though, when she wants to help and makes it worse, far worse. Use your imagination.

One particularly unpleasant day, she again stated that she wanted to leave this awful place once and for all! She hated it here and was miserable. I said, "Mom, I know you want to leave, so I'll tell you what, I will try to help you do so." And I began to research and search for an option for her.

Of course, she couldn't do what she *really* wanted: to live alone on her own. Aside from the obvious fact that she couldn't take care of herself, she had no place to go. She had lived with us for twelve years and did not have a place of her own to go to. Having bought the home she lived in the twenty years prior to that, I sold it and used the money to help us build the house we live in now. It was expensive to make it accessible for an elderly and disabled person. I can't buy her another house.

If I did find her a place, the cost of a live-in aide would be prohibitive. We were already draining her Social Security benefits to cover the increasing cost of care. She wanted her niece, Florence, to come and care for her – but Florence is not that much younger than Mom and has her own health challenges. It was not possible. So that pretty much ruled out any option for her having her own place under any circumstance.

We have two memory loss programs here in town. One I didn't care for at all – it had a bad vibe. The other was better — basically they just keep an eye on the patients as they wander in a confined environment and do what they want within the bounds of safety and respect for others. I wanted Mom engaged and active. Left alone, she retreats deeper into the delusions with no good outcome.

A third memory loss place is not built out yet — this one promises trained staff who will work with patients, not inventory them. This type of service is very expensive, but they were offering a significant discount for pre-construction commitments.

I put a deposit and waited for the construction on the new wing to be completed. Another plus here is that Mom would be the first person to live in her room. Because of the high cost she would have to share the room, but if the coupling were right, it would draw her out socially and could be highly beneficial.

Mom's CNA took her to see the assisted living facility associated with the new memory loss program. Mom loved it and raved about it in phone conversations: how beautiful it is and all the activities going on! She was excited, and we began to plan for the transition. But months later, there has been no progress at all on the construction; now they say the program may be delayed six months or more. I am exploring other options. Meanwhile, Mom is confused and making up stories in her head about what happened. I cannot explain it to her. Now she hates the place, the people: It and they are part of a new and painful delusion.

You can expect to pay around three thousand dollars monthly for a memory loss program, depending on location. Then there are add-ons depending on the level of care required: Does the patient need help taking medication, using the bathroom and maintaining hygiene, getting dressed, and grooming? Mom's needs at this point would cost about five thousand a month. She could live another two or three years, maybe more, so we're talking sixty thousand dollars a year — this is prohibitive. Mom has no supplemental insurance, assets, or savings of any sort. I hadn't planned for this at all. I assumed she would live with me until she died, in our home, where she was safe, and I could be confident of her care.

I sought advice from a counselor. The Counselor said that no matter how well intentioned the new place was, eventually the care would amount to just letting patients wander within a confined environment and do whatever they want within the bounds of safety and respect for others. She said that it would become financially overwhelming to have the staff do what the program represented they would do. Even so, she encouraged me to consider placing my mother in a program. She said since I could not afford sixty thousand a year, I should consider a place that takes state aid. She gave me a list.

I checked them out, and it was grim. They were nursing homes or looked like nursing homes. They were crowded and the elderly were still in night clothes in the middle of the day. They sat in wheelchairs in the halls staring into space. It took weeks for me to erase those images.

Mom sees her doctor every three months so he can monitor her condition. She has an Exelon Patch that he monitors as well. He didn't want to prescribe it for her, but I insisted. In my touring of programs, care providers strongly suggested that it would help her. Reluctantly, he wrote the script. He asks about it routinely. I tell him, "It doesn't fix anything, it doesn't make the dementia go away. But it does subdue the trauma she has over a given delusion."

At one point, she would get very upset when someone she believed was coming to pick her up didn't arrive. She would pace, hyperventilate, and scratch herself until she bled. The Patch helps with that: Though she still has the delusions, she is less panic-stricken and freaked out by the disappointments." He said he found that interesting.

I took her in this week. They weighed her and checked all the vitals. I reported that her appetite was less consistent and, some days, she just won't eat. She naps more and says she has a cold. He checked her breathing and said her lungs sound fine. Her temperature was normal. I reminded him she runs low. I said I felt that some things are mutating: her alertness, communication, sleep/awake patterns, and coordination. I asked if I should be doing anything differently or be recognizing some progression. He reminded me that Mom is dying and that this is her process. Our job was to care for her and keep her safe and comfortable as she travels along that path.

Mom likes the doctor. They trade Bible "promises" when she visits and talk heaven and God's grace. He is a nice man and I like him, too. I especially like that Mom likes him. I believe that he truly cares for her comfort. There have been times when he sides with her in terms of letting her do what she wants. I know he is correct. At this point, why should she do anything she doesn't want to do? On the other hand, I'm the one who has to maintain her weight, protein level, medications, etc. There are times when I wish he were more … I'm not sure … involved, helpful, supportive … — on my side once in a while.

She does have a little bit of a cough, so I began to monitor that. I noticed a while ago that she needs to be reminded to blow her nose, so she won't cough. She has lost the correlation of the nasal drip and coughing. Her temperature was normal but she (and I) usually run low, so should we be alarmed that it was normal? He didn't seem to think so. In the morning, the Earth has continued on an anticipated rotation such that the sun reappears on the horizon as expected, and we proceed.

But over the next days into weeks, she seemed to be losing it more and more. Finding words is more and more difficult for her. She is having trouble swallowing and it is evident to me that she is nearly blind.

Recently we went to see her eye doctor. He said that she was very blind and nothing more could be done for her vision. This was confirmation.

Sometimes she forgets to use her glasses. She is always losing her magnifying glass. She tells me that her Bible is not hers because it doesn't make sense. She sees things that are not there and doesn't see things that are. I wasn't sure if it was all because she just can't see well, or what, exactly.

Part of what makes this difficult is that, increasingly, I need to be able to read the tea leaves to figure out what is going on from day to day, moment to moment. Is it that she can't see? Is it that she doesn't remember the things she needs to see? Or maybe she can no longer interpret what she sees. Either way, the eye doctor confirmed that the blindness, regardless of the exact cause, was a reality.

Eating was now a matter of chasing the food around the plate, to the point that I would help her "find" the food — and this would make her mad. She would say, "I can do it myself; I have all my life!" I began selecting plate colors that had the greatest contrast with the food. Between that and the difficulty chewing, swallowing... meals are very difficult for both of us. But I'm eating just fine. In fact, I'm gaining weight at about half a pound a month. I can't seem to alter the trajectory.

Increasingly I worry about that equation on her side. I perceive that inconsistent eating is complicated by the fact that she no longer seems to know when she's hungry. She'll say she's not hungry. Then, when I get her to the table and give her something she likes, she eats it all. Sometimes she refuses to eat for a day, and I wonder if it's because she can't make the connections anymore. Maybe food tastes different to her now, maybe at times she thinks she's eating something other than what it is.

When I enter the room, I make a point of identifying myself and touching her, so she knows where I am. Her conversation is very limited; she says words that don't fit into context. I know something is going on, but I'm not sure what it is. She is in transition. But from what to what? Where is this going and how long till we get there?

I've read nearly everything available on the internet and all the literature I get at support groups and facilities. Alzheimer's disease is a death sentence because it will kill the patient eventually. Nothing can survive the death of the brain. A typical cycle is five to seven years. I figure she is almost three years in and has progressed very far along the symptom spectrum. Is there another four years, another two? I know it is late-stage dementia — and that it is likely Alzheimer's. I also know that undeterred, it will end in complete failure of mental processes and diminishment of bodily functioning, because the brain controls everything. Our family tends toward longevity, so this could be a long ride to a very grizzly end. But where are we on the journey? What's next? Why can't anyone help us? Help me?

She is more agitated, angry, frustrated, and combative. The disease causes her to hate me. Openly and aggressively she expresses her disdain for anything I do or say. The other day she tried to attack me with a letter opener — the one time I was grateful for her compromised eyesight. Everything is wrong, bad, negative, and disappointing. Her bellicose behaviors are more pointed and unrelenting. It makes it very difficult to be in the same room with her. Sometimes she won't let me be in her room. No matter what I tell myself about the disease — that this isn't really my mom — it is almost impossible not to feel pain and hurt.

Now she hates her caregiver and wants me to fire her. It is unfair, it is the disease. But she makes it hard on her when she comes. I am worried that she will just quit, then what will I do.

I have applied to the county in the hope of getting financial support to hire more caregivers so I can have respite time and to have backup in case we start losing them. Maybe the county can help me place her in a memory loss program. This proves disappointing.

They completed a form that is a time study of small events: how long does it take to do a load of laundry, a 'panty' change, meal prep, bathroom visit. We ended up getting ninety minutes a month. I laughed. Maybe I don't know how to work the system. If so, part of me is proud to claim it! But no help there. She could go into a nursing home, but there is a waiting list and no availability in our county. I sighed. Then I recalled the vapid images of neglect I'd seen in the nursing homes I visited a while back.

To be honest, some days I feel like putting her in a nursing home just to be free of this nightmare. But then the reality of that hits me right between the eyes. She will probably turn on them and accuse them of God knows what – and how will I know? Elderly, helpless people are victims of abuse, even in the best facilities. How will I know if she is being mistreated? How will I ever know?

On the other hand, I could spend all day there to care for her. Then I would know she's okay and could still go home at night and get some sleep. But the night shift: She is up all night. Would they pay attention, mind her? Sometimes staff prefer night shifts so they can escape scrutiny. But if I were there every day, I'd know. I'm getting to the point where I would take any help at all. Almost to the point where I run out into the night screaming and run till I drop!

With conversation more difficult, she is more inclined to slap me or scratch me. It reminds me of that first week after the surgery. I was giving her a bath, and all was going quite well, considering. Out of the blue, she tells me she wants to cut off my head with a knife and watch me bleed — and she said it articulately and succinctly.

I was so affected by it that I could hardly continue with the bath. I kept repeating to myself that she doesn't mean it. But with all the beheading nonsense going on in the world, it pierced my barriers and hurt – badly. It struck at the core of the feelings a beheading is designed to evoke. What a thing to say; I wasn't sure how to respond. I didn't. I finished the bath, did her hair, and helped her into bed. Then I went to my room, sat on my bed, and tried to erase the words with the television. I didn't sleep that night. I was disturbed.

I found myself considering if she could hurt me. I concluded that if

I stayed aware, she couldn't. It was more a matter of whether I would hurt her in trying to defend myself than if she could hurt me. But if she caught me off guard, she might be able to hurt me. Maybe not significantly — because her coordination and reasoning have eroded, and she is no longer formidable — but she probably could hurt me. There was a time when she could have taken me. She is small but strong and has always been clever. But not now.

It occurs to me that it is very weird to be thinking this way. This is not normal, and it is not good. I am trying to wipe it from my mind. But the words are stinging and enduring. Forget it, I say, over and over again. Then I say it again, and again...

Last night — well, early on Tuesday morning — she fell. I was awake and heard it. I went to see if she was alright. She was on the bathroom floor. Fortunately, we had placed a soft, padded covering for her protection. I checked her over: nothing broken. With the lifting belt I got her up and onto the toilet seat.   Bruises were already forming, and she had a cut on the shin bone of her right leg. I got Neosporin and a band aid. I check her all over again: nothing broken. I help her get back into bed. She is quiet the rest of the night.

Today, Wednesday, is my day away. I leave her in the CNA's care and attend to business in town. When I return, the caregiver is in the living room. As I come in the door, she says, "She threw me out of her room and won't let me back in, so I have not been able to help her. I don't know what she's doing."

I go in and greet her. She says, "Good. I need to potty." This is odd as her walker is next to her. But I think maybe she cannot see it or had to go badly and needs help. I put the walker right in front of her, but she cannot get up from the chair. I see a small flash of neon in my peripheral vision but ignore it and swing the wheelchair into place. If she has waited too long to go, she may not be able to get up without peeing. It is not unusual, but it is also somehow wrong. I help her into the chair, take her to the bathroom, and help her onto the toilet.

When she is finished, I expect her to use the rails to get up, but she cannot get up. So I help her get into the wheelchair. I half expected her to ask for her walker. I excuse the caregiver and help her get ready for bed. I need to help her at every step, far more so than usual. And all night long, she calls me to help her if she wants to get up. This is odd.

Next morning, it's still going on. I call her doctor and we go to see him in the afternoon. She is only eighty-eight pounds. Her blood pressure is slightly elevated, her pulse- ox is slightly low, her temperature is *normal*, again. She is not at all talkative as she typically is with the doctor. She is lethargic and in the wheelchair. The doctor looks her over and says that the cut on her right shin is infected. The neon is a little brighter now, but I am intent upon this discussion. I say that she doesn't usually get infections. The doctor isn't alarmed. I report her various deteriorations over the past month since our last visit. He is not moved. I ask if we should consider hospice — then I would have help monitoring all this and making decisions. He is sure we are nowhere near hospice. He prescribes antibiotics and we leave.

I pick up the antibiotics and head home. On the way, Mom starts on a tirade saying that I lied to her. That I had told her if she went to the doctor, afterward I would take her to Angelus Temple to see her students perform. I explain that Angelus Temple (which isn't there anymore) is in Los Angeles and it would take eight hours to drive there. It is already 4:00 p.m. and how in the world could we get there for a performance this evening.

Recently, she has crafted a delusion in which she has opened a school for underprivileged children. She has many people working for her and teachers who educate the children. She is involved with this delusion at the moment, so it is not surprising she is on this tangent right now. She is also really mad at me right now. She is less than articulate: It is a garbled and incoherent rant.

We arrive home, I get her inside, and it degenerates from there. All night she is worried about her children, where are they? Why won't I take her to Angelus Temple to get them? Why am I so jealous of her children and mean to her? She doesn't sleep, so I don't sleep. Whenever possible I try to get her to have yogurt or a protein drink. Her weighing only eighty-eight pounds is upsetting. I know I need to keep her protein intake as high as possible because muscle loss will negatively impact her mobility. Is this why she can't walk? Is it why she fell? Things are definitely going wacky.

On Friday, she is agitated and combative. The day passes with difficulty into the night: lots of ranting and slurring, little cooperation. She is listing to the left a little. I straighten her up but within fifteen minutes, she is listing again. She is not interested in sleep. She tells me to go to bed and leave her alone. I do so, but I'm unable to sleep.

On Saturday I have arranged for another caregiver to come and give her a sponge bath and massage. This allows Marie and I to go take care of some business and gives me a break. When we return, I am hopeful. Sure enough, Mom seems calmer and in a better mood.

I prepare some lunch, but soon am disappointed. With the caregiver gone, she resumes the bellicose attitude and behaviors. Another night of agitation and little, if any, sleep. At about 3:00 a.m., I hear a loud noise. I go to her room: She has fallen out of bed and is wedged between the bed and dressing table. I try to lift her out but wrench my back. I go get Marie to help. We get her up and see that new bruises are forming and there is a cut on the left side of her chin. I rush to treat it with an antiseptic wipe, Neosporin, and a band aid.

By morning, the chin cut is infected. Now the neon light is flashing. I thought I had cleaned it well, how could it be infected? What is going on? Maybe the antibiotics are making her flip out; clearly, they are not protecting her from infection.

Any new drug or diet ingredient whatsoever can cause the dementia to worsen. Must be the antibiotic. But why is the second cut infected? Already, within hours? What is going on?

The doctor is not in on Sunday, so I plan to call him first thing on Monday. She doesn't want to go to church. More and more often, she does not want to go. All her life she has gone to church on Sunday — and in the past three years she has gone faithfully. She loves going to church because her best friend will be there, and they sit together. Mom holds Pearl's hands in hers because Pearl is always cold, and Mom is always warm. But periodically over the past three months, she has declined to go. This, in itself, is not alarming, but it is a part of a picture that is becoming very much so.

The day goes on wIth agitation and combativeness, so much so that Marie, who usually stays out of it, intervenes. Mom doesn't give Marie much guff, so things improve. Marie talks with her for the afternoon. She reminds her how they met and talks about her home in San Juan Capistrano. Mom listens attentively, seemingly calmer and more compliant. But Marie leaves for work at 4:00 a.m. and eventually needs to go to bed.

Almost immediately, Mom gets into a delusion that her brother Frank is coming to take her home. She has been on and off this particular jag for about twenty-four hours. Now she begins to scream, "Frrraaannnk!" "FFrrraaannnk!" She continues screaming for Frank for four hours. Nothing will stop her. I try to shush her, distract her, dissuade, ask questions, get her to tell me a story, anything.

Poor Marie is trying to sleep. I do whatever I can think of to stop the screaming. By 9:00 p.m. I am frantic and on my last nerve. I've had no sleep for days, no hope in sight, and now she is screaming. I wanted to throttle her; I confess. I was frantic. I hastily rolled her out of the garage onto the driveway. I had to get out of that room, out of the house, I had to! Outside, I am calmed immediately. It is a pleasantly warm August night and there is a refreshing breeze. Overhead the edge of the galaxy is in full, glorious display: shooting stars, remnants of the latest meteor shower. I am transfixed by the wonder of this universe and instantly brought back into focus.

But she isn't. She started screaming, "FFrrraaannnk, they're killing me!" After about ten minutes of this, the neighbors called the cops — in our location, it is the sheriff's office. Two arrive and quickly catch on to what is happening. One engages her, the other asks me what they can do to help. I say that it would be helpful if they could get her to eat a yogurt – because I can put a tranquilizer in it and maybe she would sleep. They take her inside and suggest she eat a yogurt; I smash the pill and add it before they give it to her. The one deputy tells me they deal with this all the time and that I can call them to come out and help — that sometimes seeing their uniforms brings order to a situation. I thank them and they leave.

The tranquilizer does nothing whatsoever to calm her. She's not screaming anymore, but she is still agitated. At some point, I am so tired and fall asleep. I awake to a thud. She is stark naked and has fallen out of the wheelchair onto the floor. Her clothes are thrown about ... shoes, panties, and all — she can't get up.

I jump up and check for broken bones, then pick her up and set her in the wheelchair. I ask what the nakedness is all about. She says those are not her clothes, she wants her clothes. I ask if she wants to go to her room and get something to wear. She repeats that those were not her clothes. I ask questions to keep her from ranting and raving. In time, she says she has to pee; we go into her bathroom and I help her onto the toilet. When she's done, I calmly ask if she wants clean panties; she says yes. I ask if she wants a clean nighty; she says yes. I put her robe on her in the meantime.

But for the rest of Sunday night, or actually Monday morning, she struggles to get out of the wheelchair — pushing, lifting, failing, struggling, lifting. I sit transfixed and amazed. I admire her fight. I watch her in this insane endeavor and swell with awe and respect for her valiant battle against this cruel and unfair curse of Alzheimer's.

I say calmly and without emotion, as if I need to say it because *I* need to hear it — yet I'm almost certain she did not understand me: "Mom, I see you fight and I admire your resistance against what is so awful. You are so angry that this is happening, so rageful that your world has been torn from you, that you just have to rage back. I think that your aggression and your fury are reasonable. I would also feel wrath and lose my temper if this were happening to me. What you don't realize is that you take out your anger on those closest to you who only want to help you. You don't see that your allies are the very ones you attack as enemies. It makes it very difficult to help you, and it hurts. You cannot perceive this or do anything to alter it. I am sooo sorry, Mom. I wish you could comprehend that you are surrounded by people who love you. I am your daughter, I love you, and if I could, I would spare you this anguish."

She does not respond. She does not acknowledge me at all. It could be that the tranquilizer has affected her awareness. In that moment I wonder if, in her exhaustion, she was lost in some other dimension, unable to hear me or relate to me at all. At about 5:00 a.m. she went to the toilet again. When she was done, I asked if she wanted to get into bed and she said yes.

She slept at last. I did not. I was at my wits end – what was I supposed to do? At 8:00 a.m. I called the doctor's office. I was told that he was out of town and I should take her to the emergency room. I called Marie.

When Mom woke up, I made her breakfast and got her dressed. Marie came home and we took her to the ER. They checked her in and notified upstairs that they would need a room. She was fairly listless and didn't acknowledge us much at all. It was as if the angry bubble had finally burst and she had nothing left. She laid on the gurney semi curled up and quiet. I found it sad to see her contrite, even though I was relieved she was resting.

Interestingly, she checked into the ER the day after her three-year anniversary of leaving the ECU after the surgery. Life is full of weird little coincidences and correlations. I found it striking.

Finally, they told us they were going to do tests and that we should go home and get some sleep — I imagine I looked a wreck at that point. She didn't seem to know we were there, so we left. I asked them to call with any results.

It was early evening when she called — a woman who introduced herself as the ER doctor. She said they had drawn blood from Mom and found that she had rapid-onset leukemia. She said that her white cells were eighty percent corrupted and that without massive intervention, she would not survive for long.

Suddenly the neon signs were visible and clear. With a severely weakened immune system, everything is quickly compromised with infection. The doctor tells me she has damage to her heart, lungs, and liver. Considering her age, and that she has dementia, do I want to start procedures? I say no. I say that this is a miracle. This is an off ramp on the freeway to hell. The doctor says that is what she thought and that she would put her on comfort care only. She says that her legs were hurting her, so they had given her something for the pain. She was sleeping and suggested that I come to see her in the morning.

I weep. I thank god. I don't know what to do, actually. I know this is a miracle. I know that this will hurt a great deal. My mother is going to die. I know it is an out for her and I am happy for her. It is time for me to come to terms with the loss of my mother — though losing her began about a year ago. Now, here comes the ache. I breathe, then exhale. It sinks deep into my solar plexus as I let it all escape, as if there is no other air in the world and no inhale is forthcoming. Then there is a spontaneous sigh, and again the evacuation process. It is time to feel, time to deal.

Even as I experience the sledgehammer to my stomach, I am almost crippled with thinking: calculating, adding up, and sorting out. Of course, the brain and spleen work together to keep a person healthy. I wonder which part of the brain is in charge of the spleen. My mother's brain must be faulty in that region, in that section, in that location. Or some other mechanism has failed, because our family have strong immune systems. We are rarely sick and heal quickly. The brain is everything. This time maybe the degeneration attacked a critical brain function. Mom was given a means out before the bitter end of being a blob in a bed without the ability to communicate or function, waiting for the heart to stop, who knows, trapped inside… I can't even think about it. But here is the off ramp. Just like that. A mercy, from God.

The next morning, I told her that her time had finally come; that she would be going home to be with Aunt Doris, her brothers and sisters, her mom and dad, friends… and her God. She rejoiced: She was happy, and I was glad for her. But it also hurt. It didn't occur to her that it had anything to do with me. She didn't relate to me at all. I might have been a stranger telling her that. When the chaplain came in, Mom interacted with her. They prayed and read the 23rd Psalm: *…though I walk through the valley of the shadow of death… .*

I pondered the words from a brand-new perspective. It is possible to find oneself in a valley where death is not a specter to be feared. It is the valley of shadows, period — a place where nothing is clear or well defined, where nothing makes sense, everything is a reflected darkness, and death is actually the escape.

Once in the hospital, I don't think she ever ate a meal at all. I could get her to take a few sips of a protein shake, but only a few. She'd eat the ice cream for the first several days, then even that could not tempt her. If there were mashed potatoes, she'd have a taste. But her appetite was shockingly non-existent. One doctor told me that if she didn't eat, she would expire in a matter of days. And since she was on comfort care, they would not force her to eat and, of course, would not be sticking her with needles for intravenous anything. I agree. She has been tortured enough. Needles won't help her. They might help me feel that I am doing what I can to … what, provide her with food she doesn't want? Meal trays come and they go, largely untouched.

I took her teeth out to clean them and couldn't get them back in. She couldn't help me — as if she no longer remembers how to do that thing she had done so many times. I thought about calling her dentist to see if he would come to help me get them back in. Until then, her food became very soft and unappealing. So the food situation worsened quickly.

Soon, Mom is fearful. Over time, the joy of going home to heaven has been eclipsed by the prospect of going before God to be judged — and it would be heaven or hell depending on if she'd been good enough to be saved. I see it as that lifelong foreboding overwhelming any joy. The chaplain tells me it is not untypical. It is one thing to go home to glory — it is another altogether to have to face *God*. She said this would subside and that she would help Mom in the transition. I am not sure that will be possible.

Thursday morning, I am told that she will be moved to the post-acute center so the bed can be used for acute cases requiring procedures: immediate and urgent care. It began to hit me at a new level that Mom was beyond that now. One doctor told me that due to her age, it could take weeks or even months. Another said that because of the rapid onset and decline, it would only be days, a week at the outside.

I notified all her nieces, nephews, and friends. Thank goodness for Facebook, our family page, and multiple-recipient texting. When she had the hip surgery, I spent hours keeping them all up to speed. Those who were far away and had no idea what her daily life had become were alarmed and sad. Those local or who had occasion to know what the dementia had done to her and how miserable she was rejoiced for her — saddened, of course, but overwhelmed by gratitude that her trial was coming to an end. Some were so spontaneous in their rejoicing that they halted themselves and apologized, fearing I would think them insensitive. I assure them that I know the bittersweet shades of this picture and that I, too, rejoice in between heartbeats. Heartbeats that, right now, often actually hurt.

Once she moved to the post-acute center, she resumed her combative behaviors. The ECU had been disbanded and no longer existed. Many of the employees of that unit had transferred to the post-acute center. Some remembered Mom: After all, she was the star of the ECU. They were happy to see her again, then saddened by the circumstances. I wondered how they would fare under her diminished and deteriorating capacity.

I tried to tell them she would need rails on the bed. They didn't listen; they said the law didn't allow rails. I felt they were completely unprepared for Mom's condition and seemed casual and oblivious. Surely they had occasion to deal with dementia and the wandering and delusions.

The next morning, she had fallen out of bed — even more bruises and cuts. I implored them to do something. They lowered her bed near the ground and brought in a bumper bed, a kind of empty swimming pool with a rim that is hard to mount. It's low enough that even if she does get out, she will not fall far. I was satisfied, though not pleased.

But then, Mom wasn't pleased either. She battled with me all Friday. I took her out to the rose garden. Florence called my cell phone and Mom talked to her. Mom told Florence that she had committed a crime and been put in prison. Florence told her she didn't think she had committed a crime, but Mom was not persuaded.

She didn't want to go in her room or to any of the activity rooms. I took her for a roll around the facility. Food came and I tried to get her interested in at least the ice cream. But she is not having it. The nurse practitioner tells me that if she stops eating altogether, she will die in a matter of days. She has not eaten, not really, for days.

That afternoon she is caustic and tells me to take her home. I know that she doesn't mean to our house, because at our house she wanted to go "home." I realized that the home she wants is more a place where she is not demented, and that is not mine to provide.

I just try to engage her in her new, temporary home. She is angry and tells me to leave her alone if I will not help her — I should go home. Finally, a nursing assistant comes over, starts talking to her, and asks me if I needed permission to leave. I'm not sure what she means. I stand there looking at her. She says, "We got this. This is what we do. You should go." After another minute of just looking at her, I leave. I weep all the way home.

I worry that I should have brought her home and opened hospice … take care of her, whether she liked it or not. Followed by waves a mile high that wash me in inadequacy: I couldn't. I am incapable of mounting that endeavor, let alone take care of her. I am wrung out.

I tell Marie that perhaps I should stay away for a day to let her acclimate to her new digs … maybe my presence is a hindrance. The next day we bring her a change of clothes and some essentials. She is sound asleep, and we decided to leave her. We went to town and worked on a civic project to keep busy. Her best friend, Pearl, is coming to visit with her later in the day, so she won't be alone. At night I call and the desk tells me she is fine. She had been agitated during the day. She had company and now she's gone to bed.

The next morning, I take more things to her. I plan to spend time with her, see if she is more receptive, knows who I am. Maybe she'll be glad to see me; we could help her with breakfast. We'll get a better start today!

We got to her room about 7:00 a.m. I set about putting her things away, hoping to get it done before she wakes — she might be confrontational about what I had brought or not brought. I didn't want to get off on a wrong foot.

Marie says, "Nancy, is she even breathing?"

I turned. The moment I laid my eyes on her I knew she was gone. I felt for a pulse: nothing. I checked for air passing: there was not. I called a nurse; she checked for five minutes and found nothing. Mom was still slightly warm, but also cool. I figure it happened not long before we arrived.

I take her hand, stroke her hair, and say, "Mom, you finally found the way out of here! You are home now. It is over, it is ended. You are free!" Her brutal, painful, cruel path out of this life had ended.

I had always envisioned having her in my arms and her leaving straight from my arms to God's. That didn't happen, but she left from my metaphorical arms to the arms of the universe, nonetheless. I loved her very much. I might have done better at any moment. Maybe I would not have yelled at her in this moment or that. I might have been more patient, found better strategies, or made better choices. But I did the best I could at any given moment.

TIME TO DEAL

Now that it is all behind me, I will tell you: I wouldn't have had it happen any differently. I tried my best to find another way for her to be cared for; at times I was at the point of losing my own mind. The truth is, there was no way for that to happen without my having regrets. In the end, something that was cruel, awful, disturbing, and painful — that could not be avoided or set aside — happened perfectly. I don't think I would change a thing.

No, wait. There is one thing: I wish I had been better prepared for the grizzly nature of the disease before it just slapped us around. I wish I had understood what was going to happen, or what might happen, before I had to face it, handle it — improvising and lost in waves of qualm and uncertainty day after day. I wish someone had given it to me straight.

I am on a path of healing and contemplation that will probably last the rest of my life. Marie and I are re-crafting and redefining our lives and will likely be doing so for quite a while. This was huge. It will take time to unravel all the tangles and knots that formed over the past three years. I still can't sleep. Three years of just napping at night doesn't reset right away — it may take a while to get back to a normal sleep pattern. But I am more rested and relaxed. Everything is good in my heart and my mind. The rest will work itself out.

Her death certificate says she died of cardiopulmonary failure. Secondary causes are protein deficiency and advanced dementia, "probably Alzheimer's." I suppose this is an implication of the actual cause of death: the destruction of her mind, her body, and her spirit. I hope her soul survived and is in heaven, free and happy. I hope she understands what happened and is at peace knowing she was loved, very much loved. And I hope she knows that I know she loved me. I've always said that the only ones who know the mystery of death are those who have passed from life. Now she has, and now she knows.

So, is this a cautionary tale to warn you not to care for your parent who has dementia?

No, definitely not.

This is one child reaching out to another to let you know in advance what to expect and what memory loss *really* means so you know you are not alone. And to let you know that if you do undertake this, in the end you will not regret it.

I hope this can help you prepare in case the ogre comes out of left field and clunks you on your head like it did to us. Make sure your parents get supplemental insurance, including a plan that will cover this possibility. If I have a regret, it would be that I didn't sit down with Mom and convince her to start saving when she still had the capacity to make responsible decisions. When the time came, I simply didn't have the financial resources to back her for this particular crisis. The healthcare realignment will help you and it will hurt you — and you can't be sure where it will migrate. I hope you find a good set of options for your needs and circumstances.

It will be valuable and timely to begin assessing this early on so you are better prepared than were we. I should have had talks with Mom way before there was any hint of compromised reasoning. But I never did because I was sure it would not be relevant for us. But looking back in that useless hindsight, I should have answered questions like: Do we have a plan for each family member approaching 65 or older? Have we been brave and explored the "what if" scenarios? Is there money to cover memory loss care? And if not, is there a caregiver who can step in along with whatever support is available in your state and within the family?

We know people who are sensitive to this right now. They will say, "You know, I forget more than I used to do. I hope it's not a sign I'm losing it." We all become more forgetful as we age. I've always attributed it to too many frags in the memory, like a computer. Over time, little bits of code get lost or frayed. I don't think these are the most crucial signs to observe. Look for these signs:

Paranoia and/or irrational claims of persecution or loss

Recounting an event from a very different perspective than others who were present or than the individual has recounted it before.

Seeing objects or people radically differently than they appear to everyone else or not recognizing landmarks, familiar places, etc.

Insisting that something is different when it is not, such as a process, familiar book, television programs, or how the weather is forecast.

Exhibiting uncharacteristic traits of jealousy, suspicion, rude behaviors, or thoughtlessness.

If you observe any of these signs, it is time to act. Early intervention could help add time down the road. It won't fix the problem, but it may smooth the way for an easier transition into a new world, depending on the measures taken.

Also, how *you* step into this world has implications for your ability to negotiate it later. What I mean is that in the beginning, in denial, I set up dynamics that later, in acceptance, I could not reverse. Had I realized we were on that slippery slope; I would have attempted fewer rational counters to the irrational. I would have been less truth teller and more passive facilitator. I would have worked harder and more deliberately to assume the role of friend. It would have manifest like this:

Avoid arguing or confrontation

Consciously maintaining a "friendly face" and welcoming gestures

Lots of soothing touches, hugs, and pats of the hand

Dropping intellectual responses in favor of simplicity

Most important of all: keeping a sense of humor

Of course, it's hard to pretend to be what you're not and you can't always remember to do these things. But if you tend to explain things, have an answer for everything, are high energy, and struggle with nonsense, then you may be well served by adopting these suggestions as much as possible, as soon as possible.

Please do not underestimate the value of having something hit you just right and breaking down in laughter. Sometimes it tips over into nutsy or mild hysteria and you can't explain why you're laughing. But this can be an outlet that is more healing and pressure relieving than anything other than time away from the situation, and maybe more.

If you have multiple siblings, consider this: Whoever assumes the role of primary caregiver will, in time, become a bad guy in your parent's mind. In all likelihood this is unfair. The primary caregiver will carry a huge burden and other siblings should try to lighten his or her load with a meaningful hug, eye contact, a word of understanding — even though you can never truly understand. Step in whenever possible to give your sibling time off to catch her breath and refresh perspective. As you listen to your parent tell you how horrible your sibling is, remember that s/he is paying a big price for carrying this load. Be especially kind to your sibling who is sparing you from being the bad guy.

It helps to live in a small town full of understanding friends and neighbors or in a house equipped to care for a disabled person. But we didn't have anywhere near the options that exist in urban or suburban areas. There are trade-offs, as in all other aspects of life on Earth. A conversation and facing the prospect head on is as important as any other aspect of end of life planning. While everyone is of sound mind, discuss thoughts and wishes. What is the plan in the worst-case scenario? And if this cup never comes to you and your family, well good. But what if it does?

This is also a note to physicians new to this strange and uncharted landscape. It might be advisable to listen to the family and caregiver closest to the patient. These folks may be more sensitive to subtle changes than your standard norms can detect. It's not that it would have changed the outcome, but it would have been comforting to feel that our doctor was tracking more closely with us in that scary and confusing situation. When I reported that something significant and pivotal "might" be changing, would it have hurt to order that blood test on Thursday afternoon rather than in the ER on Monday? It might have alleviated a hellish, bizarre weekend, or at least helped. Perhaps hospice could have been opened that weekend and we would have had assistance. I had expressed my concerns to the doctor as early as the previous month at her regular checkup. Had hospice been engaged weeks before everything turned upside down, we might not have had to face that event on our own.

Maybe, or maybe not, but I would ask that doctors consider the observations and concerns of the caregiver who is with the dementia patient 24/7 and has known her for a lifetime. I recognize that we are all — patients, families, physicians, care professionals — trying to find our way through this disease. And this is how we navigate: We listen and consider every data point to be potentially relevant. I also recognize that the healthcare system is already highly stressed and primary care physicians are under tremendous pressure on many levels. Maybe dementia patients should be assigned a geriatric or other specialist who can track more closely patterns and anomalies and identify milestones for safely guiding everyone through this nightmare.

I understand that we could have "cried uncle" and thrown in the towel earlier, called an ambulance and taken her to the ER. It's like the deer caught in a glare. Living in a fairly crazy situation for a year with little sleep, just a couple more steps down the rabbit hole: It would take someone less compromised to know exactly which button to press, which door to open, and when enough is enough. It may prove valuable to find and keep a courageous voice of reason in your universe as it spins out of your control.

As we baby boomers enter this high-risk zone, the costs to care for the many likely to be afflicted will be prohibitive — the math is staggering. We hope for the miracle of a new treatment that can contain the damage and loss of cognitive ability. Even better, we hope for a cure that can reverse or prevent the disease.

In the meantime, baby boomers are now crossing the first threshold: aged sixty-five on their way to eighty-five. If an estimated 10 percent is even close to the risk level, it is disturbing considering how many of us boomers are alive. That means less than two decades to get a grip on this disease before the next threshold: Boomers crossing eighty-five and into the 50 percent risk category.

If a cure were in research today, it could be a decade or more before it could be made available. Unfortunately, solutions often end in failure or trips down blind alleys. It could take multiple decades to find a cure, if ever. The answer may be to seek a cure in parallel with options to buy time. Slowing the progress of the disease could be a salvation from the looming catastrophe while the quest for a cure continues.

Surely many families are travelling and will travel the path through this horrifying landscape. I am one of the first of the boomers. All my life, I have surfed the trends on the edge of what was happening. I only hope that the support systems will be more responsive in the future than they were for me and Mom. On the other hand, as a taxpayer, I question whether there is any affordable system solution.

There will be families who will elect to keep control over the quality of care so they will never be tortured by the inevitable accusations and quandary of knowing what is a delusion versus a genuine cry for help is. How would you know? Clearly, it is better to have siblings who can share the journey, share the load. Many children would want to keep their parent with them all the way, as we did. But if you opt for professional caregivers in a quality facility, there is the exorbitant cost: up to sixty-thousand dollars per year.

Whether you plan to care for a loved one yourself or to visit frequently and be part of their lives in a facility or your sibling's home, I recommend preparation to understand what is ahead and how you can cope. I suggest three books of the many available; each take very different slants on the subject of Alzheimer's disease. Together with Mom's story, they provide insights from different perspectives and nicely piece together the puzzle.

The 36-Hour Day: A Family Guide to Caring for People Who Have Alzheimer Disease, Related Dementias, and Memory Loss – Nancy L. Mace and Peter V. Rabins

Creating Moments of Joy for the Person with Alzheimer's or Dementia: A Journal for Caregivers – Jolene Brackey

On Pluto: Inside the Mind of Alzheimer's – Greg O'Brien

Support groups can be very helpful. It was the first place I learned that much of what I was trying to compensate for, assuming it was *my* problem, were actually manifestations of the disease. It is helpful to listen to others facing similar situations who can share what has and has not worked for them. Understand that a family trying to cope while their loved one is in a care facility will have a very different perspective from the raw experience of those dealing with it at home 24/7.

The professionals who organize support events and guest presenters are also helpful. But they tend to offer tactics for a person working a "shift" who gets to leave after the shift. They do have a more global point of view, the latest information, and when available: headlines.

Even if taking it on yourself is a default choice, it is a courageous one and a huge challenge, but the benefit at the end is also huge. I salute any who accept this noble mission, even if their choices are limited. It is the finest gift — a way of thanking God for your life, in a way.

Just be sure to check your baggage at the departure point. Any unresolved issues from that juncture will remain unresolved unless you handle them by yourself, within yourself. The parent will no longer be able to go there or fix anything for you.

Go into it with unconditional love for both your parent and you — or don't go there at all. Do the best you can and forgive everything else. Know and accept that there will be hurt. Everyone is different, but I think it is safe to say that you will experience anger, frustration, pain, sorrow, and feelings of inadequacy. If you are afraid, well, it is time to muster courage. Or, the fear may come in time. But I can guarantee: This will require courage.

Love your parent until the end and always remember that s/he was there for you when you were helpless and a whole lot of work! You kept her awake at night and caused worry, had accidents and made messes. Probably, you were defiant and acted like a jerk in your teens. Your parents were there for you, and now you have a chance to give back. I believe this is a gift. I hope you can see that. If not, I hope someday you will feel that it was as much a privilege as a burden.

This is a love letter to you from Mom and me in the hope that something we experienced can touch you in some dark hour and help you with this mission. If Mom were here, being herself as she was when she was younger, she would say a prayer for you and recite the perfect Bible passage for you to rely upon. From me, feeling the lump in my throat as I type, I offer the respect that swells when I think of your journey. It is my heartfelt best wishes for a bit of good luck to you and yours along the way, and the hope that your journey is both rich and favored with brevity. God bless.

9 780578 606651